5

IMPRESSIVE CREATURES

Exceptional eagles

Eagles are admired around the world for their size, flying skills and hunting ability. Here are some interesting examples of these magnificent birds.

White-bellied sea eagle – rather than screeching, this eagle honks like a goose.

White-tailed eagle – this huge eagle sometimes steals fish from otters. If the otters are wise they don't hang around to argue!

Short-toed snake eagle – with amazing eyesight, this bird can spot a snake to eat 500 metres away.

Harpy eagle – one of the largest birds of prey on the planet, feeding mainly on sloths and monkeys.

Spanish imperial eagle – an endangered species whose numbers are now recovering, a majestic rabbit-hunter that sometimes nests on electricity pylons.

Little eagle – one of the titchiest eagles, weighing less than one kilogram.

Ornate hawk eagle – a ferocious hunter that can capture prey five times its own body weight.

CONTENTS

INTRODUCTION

Nature is fantastic. Take the penguin as an example: it's a bird that can't fly, but can swim. It's slow and comical on land, but in the water it's fast, graceful and a brilliant hunter. Penguins live in some of the coldest places on the planet and around warm islands too. Emperor penguins go sledging on their bellies when they have to cross ice. Fairy penguins live in holes in the ground. Penguins are wonderful parents to their chicks. They're often not afraid of people and they make us smile!

In this book you'll find fantastic facts about whales, beetles, tigers, sharks, bushbabies, ants, eagles, hippos, wolves, otters, rats, bats and cats! As well as amazing animals and peculiar plants, there are jokes, riddles, quizzes and things to do. It's all waiting for you – dip in!

7 facts about sperm whales

1 Sperm whales have giant heads containing giant brains – the largest of any animal.

2 Most humans can only hold their breath for one to five minutes, but sperm whales can hold theirs for over an hour.

3 Sperm whales eat around a tonne of squid and fish each day.

4 People used to kill sperm whales to get a valuable substance called ambergris from their stomachs – just to make perfume!

5 Sperm whales are the largest animals with teeth. They can weigh up to 50 tonnes.

6 They are champion deep-sea divers and can reach depths of over 3,000 metres.

7 Dead sperm whales are sometimes washed up on beaches. When their bodies rot, they have been known to explode!

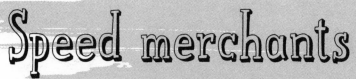

Speed merchants

You want fast animals? These creatures are RAPID!

ANIMAL	TYPE	THINGS TO KNOW	TOP SPEED
Locust	Insect	Flies in monster swarms and is always hungry.	33 kph (21 mph)
Bearded dragon	Reptile	This Australian lizard is the master of scuttling.	40 kph (25 mph)
Sailfish	Fish	Has a sharp pointed nose and a huge blue 'sail' fin.	110 kph (68 mph)
Cheetah	Mammal	Light cat, with a small head and long springy legs.	93 kph (58 mph)
Peregrine falcon	Bird	When diving for prey, this is the world's fastest living thing.	320 kph (200 mph)

Top jumps ?

Which animal can jump the highest? Well, it depends on whether you take into account body size ... You decide!

ANIMAL	HIGHEST JUMP	
Human	2.45 m	(1½ times its own body length)
Kangaroo rat	2.75 m	(25 times its own body length)
Impala	3 m	(2 times its own body length)
Tiger	4 m	(1½ times its own body length)
Brown hare	4.5 m	(8½ times its own body length)
Puma	5.5 m	(4½ times its own body length)
Flea	0.25 m	(200 times its own body length)
Copepod*	0.1 m	(50 times its own body length – through water!)

*The tiny one-millimetre copepod is a type of plankton living in the sea. It is reckoned to be the fastest and strongest animal on Earth for its size.

Hippos

Enjoy seven snappy facts about that big burly beast, the hippopotamus.

An adult hippo weighs the same as a large four-wheel-drive truck carrying five people.

Hippos often give birth underwater.

Hippos make their own sunscreen, which is red. (It's a special sticky kind of sweat that protects their skin from UV rays.)

Hippos often do explosive poos.

Hippos cannot jump.

Hippos can close their ears and nostrils when underwater.

A hippo's biggest teeth can grow as long as 50 centimetres.

Myths about gorillas

Some animals have bad reputations that are not deserved. The gorilla is one. Here are seven widespread myths (untrue ideas) about these rare and remarkable animals.

1. Gorillas are giant monkeys.
Untrue: monkeys have tails but gorillas are great apes, which do not have tails.

2. Gorillas mostly live in trees.
Untrue: gorillas live mainly on the ground.

3. Gorillas are ferocious.
Untrue: generally, gorillas are gentle and shy.

4. Gorillas are predators.
Untrue: gorillas mainly eat plants.

5. Gorillas often stand on two legs.
Untrue: gorillas walk on all fours.

6. Gorillas rampage around in gangs.
Untrue: gorillas are mainly quiet and lazy.

7. Gorillas can grow to be 20 metres tall and climb skyscrapers.
Untrue: this only happens in films.

All sorts of beetles

There are more than 360,000 types of beetle in the world. Here are a few of these incredible insects ...

BLISTER BEETLES
Their bodies contain a poisonous chemical that can blister human skin. Handle with care!

TIGER BEETLES
Some of the fastest-running insects on Earth. Champions of scurrying!

GLOW WORMS
Not worms at all, but beetles that glow in the dark.

WHIRLIGIG BEETLES
These are swimming insects which perform a frantic spinning action when alarmed.

HERCULES BEETLES
These monster beetles each have a giant horn. Their grubs weigh over 100 grams!

SQUEAK BEETLES
These mud-loving bugs make a sound by rubbing parts of their body together.

DEATHWATCH BEETLES
Their larvae (maggots) eat through wood in old houses and the adults make a clicking sound once said to be an omen of death ...

DUNG BEETLES
Some of these beasties roll animal poo into balls, bury it and then eat it. And you think your life is hard!

Balancing act

Imagine a very large see-saw. Now imagine
some animals on each end of it ...

ANIMAL

Blue whale ···
African elephant ·······························
White rhino ····································
Saltwater crocodile ····················
Yak ···
Polar bear ·····································
Tuna ···
Grey wolf ······································
Hedgehog ·······································
Black rat ···
Robin ··

WEIGHS THE SAME AS

- 2,000 adult humans
- 30 gorillas
- 10 tigers
- 550 rabbits
- 2,500 house mice
- 60 koalas
- 190 million ants
- 116 red squirrels
- 8,000 butterflies
- 40 ruby-throated hummingbirds
- 200,000 beetle mites

2,500

Things to know about giraffes

You probably know that the giraffe is the world's tallest animal. Here are some lesser known facts about this impressive creature.

When a baby giraffe is born, it falls about two metres to the ground because the mother gives birth standing up.

Giraffes were once called camelopards (a blend of camel and leopard) because they have long necks like camels and spots like leopards.

Male giraffes sometimes taste females' wee to see if they are ready to mate.

Being so tall is handy when keeping a lookout for predators such as lions and hyenas. A giraffe's main tactics for defending itself are to run away and to kick an attacker.

Giraffes sleep for less than two hours a day, and do so standing up.

Male giraffes sometimes fight by hitting each other with their necks and heads.

Let's talk

Just like humans, animals communicate with each other all the time, and they do this in a huge number of ways. Here are just a few examples.

Sounds

☛ Many monkeys screech to signal that predators, like chimps or eagles, are around.

☛ Whales 'sing' underwater to pass on information to each other.

☛ Crickets rub their wing covers together to produce a range of sounds.

☛ Asiatic wild dogs whistle to one another over long distances.

☛ Some gorillas hum to their family members when it's feeding time.

Colours

☛ Glow worms (called fireflies in the USA) produce light so they can signal to each other.

☛ The male cuttlefish can change the patterns on its skin. It has a special pattern it uses when it wants to attract females.

☛ The female olive baboon's bottom turns pink when it's ready to mate.

Movement

☛ Honey bees perform a waggle dance to spread news about flowers and nectar.

☛ Wallabies drum their feet on the ground to give a danger warning.

☛ Mole rats bang their heads against underground tunnels to send signals to their pals.

The world of bees

Bees are not only fascinating insects but they are also vitally important to the survival of human beings. Read on and you'll find out more ...

Many important crop plants around the world are pollinated by bees, including kiwi fruit, cashews, almonds, raspberries, turnips, melons, cucumbers, apples, avocados, plums and blueberries. We depend on bees for all of these foods and many others.

There are over 20,000 different kinds of bee, including whole families of bumblebees, honey bees, cuckoo bees, mason bees, sweat bees, mining bees and leafcutter bees.

Honey bees' wings move up and down 230 times a second – creating the famous buzz.

Honey bees live in large colonies dominated by the queen, who produces all of the eggs. When a queen bee dies, workers select a larva (newly hatched grub) to be the next queen. They then feed it a special food called royal jelly so that it can develop into an egg-laying ruler.

Not all bees live in colonies and make a large colony nest. Some species are solitary and make a small nest in a hole in the ground, for example.

Only female bees sting. Honey bees die if they sting. The queen is an exception, but she rarely leaves the hive so it is unusual for her to use her sting anyway.

Africanised honey bees can be aggressive and have been known to chase people for 400 metres.

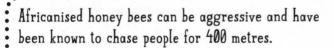

Bees swarm when they move nests. Thousands of worker bees surround and protect the queen while scout bees fly out looking for new nest sites. Swarms can be captured by beekeepers using a bee vacuum!

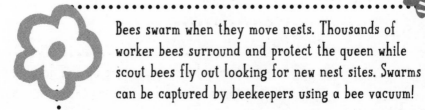

Bears

Here are six tidy facts about bears.

1. There are no bears in Africa.

2. Newborn polar bears are the size of rats.

3. A brown bear is as fast as a horse over a short distance.

4. Pandas have two thumbs on each paw.

5. Some black bears are white (these are very rare).

6. Hibernating bears sometimes eat nothing for six months.

Driver ants

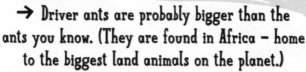

There are more than 12,000 known species of ant in the world (and some people think there may be another 8,000 not yet identified), but one to be given extra respect is the driver ant. Here's why:

→ Driver ants are probably bigger than the ants you know. (They are found in Africa – home to the biggest land animals on the planet.)

→ There can be as many as 20 million driver ants in a single colony.

→ The ants are blind but fearless, travelling in long, living highways.

→ Driver ants overpower and attack any creature in their path: scorpions, crabs, frogs, lizards and even tethered cows!

→ The ants cut up the prey and carry it back down the column to share it out.

→ Giant biting soldier ants protect the workers.

→ Driver ants don't build permanent nests, but instead keep moving all the time.

→ They can lift up to 50 times their own weight. (That's like a five-year-old child picking up a car.)

→ A driver colony will capture and consume 30,000 insects a day.

Remarkable parents

Some animals do astonishing things when they look after their young. Here are some varied examples from across the animal kingdom.

Mother cheetahs spend 18 months training their cubs to hunt while also protecting them from predators by hiding them and moving them all the time.

Orangutan babies don't let go of their mothers at all for the first year of their lives. Altogether they stay with their mums for eight years.

The strawberry poison dart frogs found in the rainforests of Central America really look after their young. The father pees on the eggs daily to keep them moist before the tadpoles hatch. Then the fearless mother carries the little tadpoles from the dangerous forest floor up into trees to tiny pools of water to keep them safe.

Octopuses will sometimes watch their eggs so carefully over many weeks that they don't even eat. In some cases, they can die from weakness once the eggs have hatched.

Parent alligators protect their little ones from danger by keeping them in their mouths while predators (mainly other large alligators) are about.

An emperor penguin will eat nothing for two months and carry its egg around on its feet to ensure the chick inside is kept warm in freezing Antarctica where it lives.

Clownfish parents spend hours fanning their young with their fins so the little ones receive oxygen-rich water, which will help them to survive.

Rheas are large flightless birds that live in South America. The female rhea lays the eggs but the male keeps them warm and safe and then raises the chicks on his own.

STRANGE AND STRANGER

Animals that only eat one thing

You might think these creatures have a very boring diet – but they seem to like it!

ANIMAL	ONLY EATS
Giant panda	bamboo shoots
Shipworm	wood
Koala	eucalyptus leaves
Worm snake	earthworms
Monarch butterfly caterpillar	milkweed
Raider ant	other ants
Bedbug	blood
Dung beetle	poo

New discoveries

New species of animals are being discovered all of the time. Of course they're not really new – it's that we've only just noticed them! Here are some especially interesting ones.

Pulsing sea slug
Found in 2015, these are unlike any other slugs you've seen: electric blue with dangly things!

Hog-nosed vampire rat
First seen in Indonesia in 2013, this wacky little rodent has extra-long, Dracula-like fangs.

Glow-in-the-dark turtle
In 2016, a rare hawksbill sea turtle was filmed glowing red and green in the deep ocean. Oo-er!

Bird-eating spider
In 2017, Brazilian researchers reported three new types of hairy spider that feast on birds and bats.

Skywalker hoolock gibbon
New mammals are rarer than new insects or sea creatures. Scientists who tracked down this gibbon in a Chinese rainforest were also Star Wars fans, announcing its excellent name in 2017.

Pigbutt worm
Hmmmm, discovered in 2006, this is a hazelnut-sized deep-ocean dweller that looks, well, like a porker's rear. Nice.

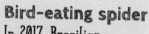

Things that snakes have swallowed

Many big snakes can open their jaws amazingly wide to allow them to swallow large animals like baby deer. Occasionally, snakes eat something extreme ...

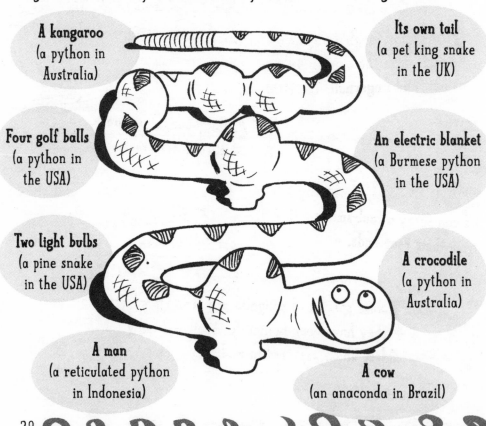

A kangaroo
(a python in
Australia)

Its own tail
(a pet king snake
in the UK)

Four golf balls
(a python in
the USA)

An electric blanket
(a Burmese python
in the USA)

Two light bulbs
(a pine snake
in the USA)

A crocodile
(a python in
Australia)

A man
(a reticulated python
in Indonesia)

A cow
(an anaconda in Brazil)

Pangolins

Pangolins are a type of anteater covered in scales. Here are seven choice facts about these armoured mammals.

1 Pangolins' tongues can be as long as 40 centimetres and are covered in sticky mucus for scooping up termites.

2 Pangolins roll into a ball when threatened.

3 Pangolins' tough scales are made from the same substance as hair and fingernails (keratin).

4 Many pangolins can climb trees.

5 When attacked, some pangolins can spray a foul-smelling liquid from their rear ends.

6 Pangolins have no teeth.

7 Some species of pangolin are endangered because they have been hunted for their meat and for their scales, which are used in medicines.

Precious poo!

When millions of animals gather in one place there is going to be a lot of plop! But surprisingly, this can be quite useful.

In the early 1800s, sailors came across islands near Peru where huge colonies of seabirds had left colossal piles of droppings, over 50 metres deep. This piled-up dung, called guano, was a very valuable fertiliser and so was collected and then bought by farmers around the world. The bird poo made some people very rich!

Guano is also found in caves where bats roost. In the 1930s, a large cave was discovered in Arizona, USA, containing nearly 1,000 tonnes of stinky bat poo. The ancient poo was mined until it was all gone.

A cow produces around 30 kilograms of manure each day (that's around 11 tonnes a year). This dairy dung doesn't go to waste, however – it's usually spread around farmland where it helps plants to grow. Chicken manure is also used in this way (although hens poo a lot less than cows!).

Cattle droppings are also used as a fuel in some countries, including India. The cow pats are dried in the sun and then burned to cook food.

In some parts of the world, animal poo is mixed with mud and straw to make a cheap building material. Millions of people live in simple houses with 'mucky' walls!

Animal poo is also collected to produce biogas. This gas can be burned to generate electricity.

Whales do REALLY big poos! Surprisingly these giant doo-doos help to make the world's oceans richer in life. Many fish and other sea creatures eat the nutrients the whale waste contains. Yuck!

There is a poo museum near Piacenza in Italy and another on the Isle of Wight, UK. Some people pay to see poo!

Blue!

Blue is one of the rarest colours in the animal kingdom. Here are some blue beasts.

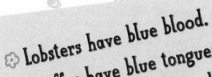

- ❀ Lobsters have blue blood.
- ❀ Giraffes have blue tongues.
- ❀ Some damselflies have blue bodies.
- ❀ Sclater's lemurs have blue eyes.
- ❀ Holly blue butterflies have blue wings.
- ❀ Blue poison dart frogs have blue skin.
- ❀ Hyacinth macaws have blue feathers.

How many legs?

Snake	0	Crab	0	Millipede	40–750
Bird	2	Woodlouse	14		
Coypu	4	Centipede	30–354		
Cockroach	6				
Spider	8				

Sea shells: who has the biggest?

Oyster	36 cm
Triton's trumpet	55 cm
Florida horse conch	60 cm
False trumpet sea snail	99 cm
Noble pen shell	120 cm
Giant clam	137 cm

Microbe madness

Microbes are everywhere, including inside us. In fact, we can't last long without them. Here are seven surprising snippets of info about these very small living things.

1 The smell of rain after a storm is caused by bacteria.

2 Used coins and banknotes are covered in microbes.

> Microbes such as bacteria are living things so small that they can only be seen through a microscope — which is why we have room for trillions of them in our bodies.

3 An average adult human body contains around 0.2 kilograms of bacteria — about the same weight as a large banana.

4 Micro-organisms on our skin break down sweat and this can lead to an unpleasant pong: body odour.

5 In 2012, scientists studied the belly buttons of 60 people and counted a total of 2,368 types of bacteria.

6 Hens' eggs have a natural coating which protects them from bacteria. Washing the eggs means that they are more likely to be infected.

7 Human poo is mostly made up of water and microbes, some dead, some alive.

Crabs

Crabs are animals of the crustacean group, famous for their shells, claws and for walking sideways! This is your guide to these highly specialised scuttlers.

○ Crabs have ten legs: the same number as lobsters, prawns, shrimp and crayfish.

○ Unlike mammals and many other animals, crabs have their skeletons on the outside of their bodies.

○ **The smallest crab is the pea crab at just three to four millimetres (the size of a small pea, in fact).**

○ The largest crab in the world is the Japanese spider crab, which can measure a stupendous 5.5 metres from claw to claw!

○ **The most powerful crab in the world is the coconut crab. Its big claws can crush coconuts, and scientists who tested them discovered that their grip is nearly equal in force to a lion's bite.**

○ The yeti crab is very strange indeed. It has no eyes, hairy legs and lives very deep in the ocean, eating bacteria that grows on its chest hairs.

Clever crabs

There are thousands of species of crab – here's a list of some of the more unusual ones:

- Hairy orange hermit
- Spiny mud crab
- Umbrella crab
- Atlantic ghost crab
- Lady crab
- Graceful decorator crab

- Velvet crab
- Arrow crab
- Electric blue leg hermit crab
- Nimble spray crab
- Pom-pom crab
- Depressed rubble crab

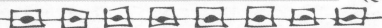

Starfish

These beautiful sea creatures are remarkable in many ways. Here are eight rather satisfying facts about them:

1. Starfish are not fish. Unlike fish they have no gills or tails, although they do live in the sea.

2. Starfish are also called sea stars. There are about 2,000 types of them in the world's oceans.

3. Most starfish have five arms but some have 40!

4. Starfish move on hundreds of tiny tube feet but they are not quick – it typically takes them seven minutes to walk a metre.

5. If a starfish loses an arm to a hungry predator, it can just grow a new one.

6. Don't touch a starfish if you find one: some of them are protected by sharp spines.

7. Starfish can push their stomachs out through their mouths to eat seashell creatures.

8. Starfish have no blood. None. But they do have a really small eye at the end of each arm.

Sponges

If you've always wanted to know about sponges, you're in the right place. If you haven't, then read on anyway because they are fascinating things ...

1. Sponges are animals but they have no head, brain, eyes, nerves or any organs.

2. Sea sponges don't move around, which is just as well as they have no arms or legs!

3. Sea sponges live mainly on the ocean floor, although some are found in lakes and rivers too.

4. Biologists used to think that sea sponges were plants. Now they are classed as animals because they need to eat to create energy, whereas plants make their own energy from the sun.

5. Sponges are covered in thousands of tiny holes that hold water.

6. Sponges feed by filtering water for tiny organisms. A large sponge can filter enough water in a day to fill a small swimming pool.

7. Sea sponges have been harvested by divers for centuries. They cut off a piece of sponge so that the rest will regrow on the seabed. Once the hard outer layer is removed, the soft insides can be used for washing and skincare.

Animals that can predict the future?

For many centuries people have noticed that animals can detect an approaching natural disaster. Their sharper senses often tell them what is about to happen, as these examples show.

In 2004, on the island of Sumatra, a group of elephants near the coast began trumpeting unexpectedly and then started heading for the nearby hills. Very soon after this a huge tsunami (giant wave) struck coasts all around the Indian Ocean, causing widespread devastation.

In 2009, scientists observed a colony of 96 toads leaving their home pond in L'Aquila, Italy. A day later an earthquake hit the area.

In 1975, in the city of Haicheng, China, many people saw hibernating snakes emerge from their winter burrows to flee the area. A few weeks later the town was hit by a big earthquake.

In 2011, researchers were studying groups of goats grazing on the slopes of Mount Etna, a volcano in Italy. They discovered that the goats became nervous and started moving around much more just before the volcano erupted.

In 2014, a group of scientists in the USA were tracking the migration flights of small birds called golden-winged warblers. Unexpectedly the birds headed south, away from their usual breeding grounds, days before a giant storm hit the area, causing huge amounts of damage.

Animal mutations

Occasionally, animals are born with unusual characteristics. These creatures are rare and often don't live for long.

In 2009, a **snake** with a clawed foot was found in China. Snakes normally have no feet or legs at all.

In 2008, an **octopus** with six legs instead of the usual eight was caught off the coast of Wales.

In 2012, scientists in India discovered a group of **white crocodiles.**

In 1999, a **black rat snake** was born with two heads.

In 2016, a **piglet** with eight legs was born in Argentina.

In 2004, some children in a nursery in England found a **frog** with three heads.

PLACES WITH TALES TO TELL

Strange places to live

Some animals live in holes, some live in trees, some live in water and some live in very peculiar places ...

Yeti crab	Lives on the seabed over two kilometres deep where there is no light.
Eyelash louse	Spends its life on other animals' eyelashes.
Remora fish	Attaches itself to a shark and stays there.
Nematode worm	Lives in caves and gold mines 3,000 metres below the Earth's surface.
Tetramorium inquilinum	An ant that lives on the back of a larger ant.
Hookworm	Makes its home in a human's guts.
Pearlfish	Lives in a sea cucumber's bottom. Really.

41

Animals in unexpected places

We expect to find forest animals in forests, sea creatures in the sea and desert dwellers in the desert. But just occasionally, wildlife turns up in surprising places ...

In Ottawa, Canada, in 2014, a bus driver found a fox asleep on one of the seats of a parked bus that had been left with its door open. Foxes are now common in cities around the world.

In the 1980s, a wealthy criminal gang boss in Colombia built his own private zoo, which included four hippos. The animals escaped, however, and began to live and multiply in the wild along a local river. Usually wild hippos are only found in Africa.

In 2015, police in New York chased a strange creature through the streets of the city. It was a coyote. Coyotes usually roam plains, forests, mountains and deserts, not cities. The beast was filmed but it eventually gave officers the slip.

Sheerness in Kent, UK, is home to some unexpected beasts: yellow-tailed scorpions. The scorpions are small but they still sting. They live in cracks in the rocks and stones around the town's docks.

In 2007, a huge flood in Australia left some river and sea animals stranded in odd places as the water receded. These included ten large bull sharks that ended up in a lake on a golf course.

In 2014, villagers in Sri Lanka were amazed when hundreds of fish fell out of the sky during a storm. Scientists think that they were sucked out of ponds by a mini-tornado.

43

Sumatra

Sumatra is a very large tropical island in South East Asia. It is home to an astonishing variety of unusual and rare animals, including these:

Slow loris

Combine big eyes, a toxic bite, a forceful grip, two tongues and the ability to keep very still and you have a slow loris.

Sun bear

This is the smallest of all bears. It's black, shy and wild about honey. Sun bears even eat the bees!

Water monitor

A scary-looking lizard that can grow up to two metres long. One of its favourite foods is live chicken.

Tapir

The tapirs found on Sumatra are big black-and-white mammals with long floppy noses. They are only afraid of humans and tigers.

Bearcat

Well, it's not a bear or a cat. Also called a binturong, it is a type of civet, which is a family of mammals not closely related to bears or cats at all. Surprisingly, bearcats smell of popcorn.

Clouded leopard

This is a very hard-to-spot big cat with beautiful markings. It's a spectacular climber – in the local language, its name means 'tree tiger'.

Golden silk orb-weaver

This is a giant of a spider, with the female having a body measuring three to five centimetres and reaching 15 centimetres overall (including legs). The teeny male is often about eight times smaller than the female.

Invaded by nature!

Sometimes animals break out from their normal habitats and pop up in places where we just don't expect to find them.

Monkeys

The city of New Delhi in India is often overrun by monkeys called macaques. They are sacred to Hindus and are fed twice a week by local people – but they often also stage raids on market stalls, pinching large amounts of food and other items.

Deer

Nara in Japan is a town famous for the 1,200 deer that roam through the streets. They are completely tame and they particularly enjoy being fed crackers.

46

Rats

The uninhabited island of Montecristo in Italy was recently infested by huge numbers of rats. The rats have now gone and other wildlife is thriving once more.

Green iguanas

The small island of Grand Cayman in the Caribbean Sea is home to around 500,000 green iguanas. These large lizards, which can grow up to two metres long, were once kept as pets, but they escaped into the wild and started multiplying rapidly.

Chickens

Kauai Island in Hawaii, USA, is populated by oodles of wild chickens. The birds have no predators and so can breed freely. They are now a tourist attraction.

Bears

The small town of Luchegorsk in eastern Russia was under siege by bears in 2015. After a season of bad growing conditions, the bears' natural forest foods ran out and they were forced to search the town for something to eat. Several people were attacked by bears in the streets.

47

No crocs live here

Large continents have all sorts of wildlife, of course, but islands – especially small ones – often have only a few native species. In some cases other animals have been introduced by humans (usually with disastrous consequences) but here are islands lacking some surprising creatures:

ISLAND	HAS NO
Hawaii	rabbits
Iceland	snakes
Tuvalu	deer
New Zealand	crocodiles
Grenada	foxes
Ireland	moles
Falklands	frogs
Easter Island	mammals at all

BEWARE!
What to do if attacked!

Nearly all wild animals are scared of people and stay away from us whenever possible. However, now and again we really get in their way. Here's what to do if they decide to go for you.

Wasp: move away slowly.

Goose: stay facing the goose, stare at it and back away slowly.

Gull: hold up something above your head like a bag or stick.

Brown (grizzly) bear: pretend to be dead.

Swarm of bees: run away fast and get indoors.

Python: if trapped in its coils, bite the snake's tail or hit it with a hard object.

Shark: stay facing the shark and whack it on the nose.

Lion: do not run; stand, wave your arms, shout loudly and throw an object at it.

Crocodile or alligator: run and keep running.

Fancy a bite?

Some animals have teeth, and some don't. The ones that do have all kinds of startling incisors, molars and more. Enjoy this interesting information about the world of bitey beasts!

The spinner dolphin has over 200 teeth – imagine how long a check-up at the dentist would take!

Baboons have nasty five-centimetre-long fangs (canines), which are mainly for show. Lions have canines seven centimetres in length – those are certainly not just for show and you should avoid them at all costs.

The tropical titan triggerfish has a brutal bite with teeth that can crush hard coral. It has been known to attack divers who get too close.

Elephants' tusks are the longest teeth of any animal, sometimes over three metres long and weighing 60 kilograms each.

Bull sharks have 50 rows of teeth. They lose teeth all the time when aggressively biting their prey, but their clever in-mouth tooth replacement system produces new ones continuously.

The narwhal is a strange whale that has a single long tusk with an amazing twisted appearance. This spear-like tooth, usually around two metres long, actually grows through the animal's lip.

The babirusa or deer-pig of Indonesia has huge curved teeth that grow out of its jaw and back towards its head. If the deer-pigs don't grind these tusks down, the tusks can pierce their own skull. Ouch!

BEWARE!

Perilous plants

Most plants are harmless, but not these
cunning green fiends. BEWARE!

Giant hogweed
This three-metre-high weed has sap that makes skin
burn severely in sunlight and can even cause blindness.

Honey locust tree
It sounds lovely, doesn't it? But watch out for
this bush's ten-centimetre thorns, which can
go right through the soles of your shoes!

Coconut palm
When a coconut falls from
a tree and you are right
underneath, it can give you a
headache at best and sometimes
much worse ...

Strangler fig
A giant climber that grows up trees and blocks out their light, often causing them to die and rot.

Tree nettle
An extra-nasty monster nettle from New Zealand that grows up to three metres in height and is covered in spikes with dangerous toxins.

Deadly nightshade
This innocent-looking woodland plant has shiny black berries that can kill if eaten. So stay away!

Machineel tree
Even just sheltering beneath this weird tree can give you a painful rash because of the powerful chemicals in its poisonous sap.

Sea monsters

The oceans of our planet are home to some strange, big, menacing and hungry creatures: you have been warned!

LAMPREY
This fish is a parasite that attaches itself to larger fish and sucks their blood. Nice.

TORPEDO RAY
A seabed-dwelling flatfish that can fire painful electric shocks when touched. Avoid.

SEA SNAKE
A sleek champion swimmer with a deadly venomous bite. Yikes.

SAND DEVIL
This small flat shark hides on the seabed and bites when disturbed. Ouch!

LEOPARD SEAL
A penguin-eating, sharp-toothed, heavyweight hunter of cold waters. Ooh.

PORTUGUESE MAN O' WAR
It looks like a jellyfish but it is really a whole colony of nasty stinging creatures. Pain!

GIANT PACIFIC OCTOPUS
A 200-kilogram, nine-metre-wide brute that can crush thick shells and munch large fish. Eek.

WHALE SHARK
Larger than a bus, with a gigantic mouth – just as well it has no teeth. Phew!

Scary-sounding creatures

These animals don't sound too friendly but they are all REAL!

- Killer whale
- Vampire finch
- Ghost crab
- Stingray
- Bullet ant
- Firefly
- Blood shrimp

- Deathwatch beetle
- Komodo dragon
- Tongue-eating louse
- Poison dart frog
- Thorny devil

What a defence!

The animal world is full of predators trying to catch and eat prey, and full of prey not wanting to be eaten! The animals below have come up with clever ways to protect themselves.

Opossum
Pretends to be dead, craftily letting out an unpleasant smell of decay.

Horned lizard
Squirts blood out of its eyes.

Cereal leaf beetle
Makes itself a less popular meal by coating its body in poo.

Bombardier beetle
Sprays a mix of very hot, toxic chemicals out of its bottom.

Hagfish
Produces astonishing amounts of choking slime when bitten.

Malaysian ant
Has a poison sac which it can explode if attacked.

Salamander
Can leave behind its waggling tail to confuse predators.

Pangolin
Curls into a ball, covering its body in extra-sharp, hard scales.

American bullfrogs

These bullfrogs are legendary for eating just about anything they can get in their mouths. Here is a list of things they like to munch:

Tadpoles

Birds Slugs

Mice

Beetles

Spiders Snails

Bats

Crayfish Lizards Flies

Fish Other bullfrogs Snakes

57

Sneaky disguises

Camouflage is all about hiding, and many animals are experts at it. Some do it so that they won't be eaten, others use it to hide from their poor unsuspecting prey ...

Lacy scorpionfish

It looks exactly like a piece of sea coral, but it has a very big mouth — so be careful if you are a little fish.

Stick insects

These skinny guys are old masters not only at blending into their surroundings but also at keeping still when danger is near.

Dresser crab

This cunning creature picks up bits of coral and sponge and sticks them on its body so that it cannot be seen.

Tawny frogmouth

This Australian bird looks so much like a broken tree branch that it's almost impossible to spot when it's keeping still.

Owl butterfly

This crafty insect has big spots on its wings that look like owls' eyes. These are enough to frighten away small predators.

Dead leaf butterfly

Well, it looks like a dead leaf. Really, really like a dead leaf. Clever.

Octopus

The octopus is probably the world champion of camouflage because it can change the colours, patterns and shapes on its skin to match nearly any background. Look up some videos of it doing this incredible costume change.

Horns

Some animals have horns, some have antlers and some have other knobbly bits sticking out of their heads! Here is your quick guide.

Is it a horn?

Horns are permanent pointed features with a live bone core and covered in keratin (the substance your fingernails are made of).

Rhino horns?

Unlike the horns of sheep or cattle, rhino horns have no bone inside.

Longest horns?

One Asian water buffalo measured in 1955 had horns measuring 4.2 metres from tip to tip.

Most horns?

Some sheep and cattle have four horns and some goats have eight horns.

Insect horns?

Some beetles have growths that look like horns but these are part of their outer skeleton.

Uses of horns?

Animals use horns for defence, to attract a mate and to fight off rivals.

What about antlers?

Antlers are branched, unlike horns, and formed of dead bone. They are shed each year and regrown.

Tusks?

Tusks are giant teeth, so very different to horns.

61

BEWARE!

Animals with

weapons!

Some creatures are armed and dangerous, so watch out! Many animals have weapons to defend themselves against predators and the hunters are usually armed for attack.

WEAPON	ANIMAL EXAMPLES
Powerful bite	hyena, crocodile, moray eel
Sting	scorpion, jellyfish, stingray
Horns	wild cattle, cape buffalo, rhino
Strong claws	Kodiak bear, osprey, panther
Venomous bite	black mamba, Brazilian wandering spider, blue-ringed octopus
Deadly crush	boa constrictor, python, anaconda
Squirt acid	wood ant, oogpister beetle, whip scorpion
Sprays foul-smelling liquid	skunk, striped polecat, hoopoe
Sharp spines	hedgehog, porcupine, sea urchin

Here are some more unusual animal weapons:

WEAPON	ANIMAL EXAMPLES
Spreads slime	hagfish
Fires sticky spit	spitting spider
Has a muscular nose for bashing	elephant
Squirts water jet	archer fish
Has a 80 kph punch	mantis shrimp
Explodes its body	Malaysian ant
Has a sticky web	spider
Gives an electric shock	electric eel
Fires a sonic shockwave	pistol shrimp
Flicks irritating hairs	Mexican redknee tarantula
Has giant crushing claws	Coconut crab

Cannibal animals

Some living things have an ungallant habit of eating their own kind ...

King snake
This hungry reptile loves nothing better than to feast on other snakes. It's immune to their venom too.

Amazon catfish
These beasts of the giant river can grow over two metres long. They eat any fish they come across.

Sand tiger sharks
These gruesome sea monsters eat smaller brothers and sisters while still in the womb!

Sticklebacks

These small fish will sometimes eat their own eggs. Well, it saves going to the shops!

Bullfrogs

Famous for eating anything they can get in their mouth. Unfortunately this may include their own tadpoles.

Lobsters

Big lobsters sometimes eat smaller lobsters. It's not the best way to make friends ...

Praying mantis

After mating, the female eats the male. Well, it saves having to get him a birthday card ...

Black lace-weaver spider

When baby lace-weavers are three or four days old they eat their mother. Not much gratitude there ...

Unusual snakes

Snakes are very interesting animals for many reasons. Here are some of the stranger snakes found across the planet.

Golden sea snake

Scientists have discovered that this swimming serpent has light detectors in its tail. You could say that it can see from both ends!

Tentacled snake

A sneaky river snake with dangling motion-detectors on its head. When hunting it pretends to be a dead tree branch so it can grab unsuspecting passing fish with ridiculous speed.

Spitting cobra

Stay well away from this one: it can spray extra-nasty venom from its fangs up to two metres in distance. The venom can blind a person if it gets into their eyes.

Flying snake

A truly amazing snake that will hurl itself off a high tree if startled then glide down to the ground, writhing its flattened body in a series of graceful S-bends.

Barbados thread snake

It's ten centimetres long, as thin as spaghetti and is the smallest snake in the world. Being so tiny, the female only lays a single egg.

Tiger keelback

This Asian snake likes to dine on poisonous toads. Not only is the tiger keelback immune to the toads' poison, but the cheeky reptile also stores the venom in special neck glands to use for its own defence. Waste not, want not ...

WORLDWIDE WILDLIFE
How to say 'lion' in 15 languages

Here's your chance to be a multilingual smartypants nature expert!

- ⊙ **Afrikaans** leeu
- ⊙ Croatian lav
- ⊙ **Danish** løve
- ⊙ French lion
- ⊙ **German** Löwe
- ⊙ Hungarian oroszlán
- ⊙ Indonesian singa
- ⊙ Irish leon
- ⊙ Italian leone
- ⊙ **Latvian** lauva
- ⊙ Polish lew
- ⊙ **Spanish** león
- ⊙ Swahili simba
- ⊙ **Turkish** aslan
- ⊙ Xhosa ingonyama

Animals found in only one place

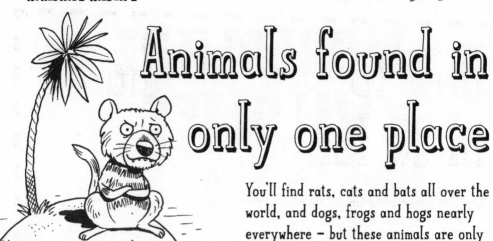

You'll find rats, cats and bats all over the world, and dogs, frogs and hogs nearly everywhere – but these animals are only native to one island or group of islands:

ANIMAL	TYPE	ONLY LIVES IN
Kiwi	bird	New Zealand
Lemur	mammal	Madagascar
Sri Lanka blossom krait	reptile (snake)	Sri Lanka
Platypus	mammal	Australia
Java mouse-deer	mammal	Java (Indonesia)
Scilly bee	insect	Isles of Scilly (UK)
Matschie's tree kangaroo	mammal	Papua New Guinea
Spectacled flowerpecker	bird	Borneo (Malaysia, Brunei, Indonesia)
Tasmanian devil	mammal	Tasmania (Australia)
Blotched salamander	amphibian	Japan

How to say 'elephant' in 15 languages

You just never know when this might come in handy ...

- **Afrikaans** — olifant
- **Filipino** — elepante
- **Finnish** — norsu
- **French** — éléphant
- **German** — Elefant
- **Hausa** — giwa
- **Hindi** — haathi
- **Malay** — gajah
- **Italian** — elefante
- **Luxembourgish** — Nitrater
- **Slovak** — slon
- **Somali** — marpodiga
- **Spanish** — elefante
- **Swahili** — tembo
- **Uzbek** — fil

Your monkey guide

Everyone loves a monkey — and here you can find out about the amazing variety of these hairy, bouncy, tree-loving mammals.

Allen's swamp monkey

A greenish-grey primate from the Congo in Africa that can swim among the swamps where it searches for fruit and worms to eat. It has slightly webbed hands and feet.

Booted macaque

This strongly built monkey is found only on the island of Sulawesi in Indonesia. It has grey limbs and a darker body, which gives the impression that it is wearing long boots.

Yellow baboon

These are large monkeys with long snouts, which is why the word baboon comes from the Greek for 'dog-head'. They live in large troops of around 200 and are found across central Africa. Some farmers regard them as pests because of their raids on food crops.

Drill

An endangered monkey from West Africa. Male drills are around twice as large as females. They have dark silvery fur with pink-and-blue bottoms.

Buffy-headed marmoset

This rare monkey has a curious woolly head and lives in the rainforest of Brazil. It is very small, usually weighing less than half a kilogram, and is a favourite prey of big cats, big snakes and big birds. If a marmoset sees a snake it will raise an alarm, screeching so that others can gather and mob the attacker.

Three-striped night monkey

This primate is one of a group of nocturnal monkeys, which means they are active at night. For this reason they are sometimes called owl monkeys. It has huge eyes and white face markings that resemble stripes.

Emperor tamarin

This small South American monkey is notable for its spectacular moustache, which led to it being named after the German emperor Wilhelm II who favoured a giant 'tache' of his own. Tamarins live most of their lives in trees, rarely visiting the forest floor because of the presence of predators.

Atlantic titi

This mysterious monkey lives in a small pocket of the coastal forests of Brazil, where it spends its time looking for fruit and seeds to eat – although these monkeys have also been observed eating soil, for unknown reasons. The titi can be recognised by its black face and brown fur.

How to say 'cat' in 14 languages

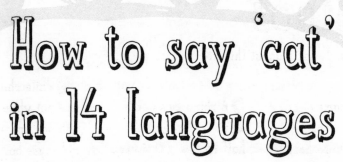

Cats are found all over the world and every country has a word for this clever, adaptable, graceful hunter.

- **Bosnian** **mačka**
- Danish kat
- Estonian kass
- Filipino pusa
- **Finnish** **kissa**
- French chat
- **German** **Katze**
- Hawaiian popoki

- Hungarian macska
- **Lithuanian** **kate**
- Italian gatto
- **Maltese** kot
- **Spanish** **gato**
- Welsh cath

Rhinos

Eight handy facts about this wondrous beast of Africa:

1 The name rhinoceros means 'nose horn'.

2 A rhino can weigh up to three and a half tonnes – the same as three small cars.

3 White rhinos are not white, and black rhinos are not black. (They're both grey.)

4 Rhinos can 'read' poo: they can tell from the smell if a pile of rhino dung has come from a male or female rhino and whether it was old or young.

5 The Javan rhino is said to be the world's rarest land mammal. There are only around 60 left on the planet.

6 The scientific name of the Indian rhino is *Rhinoceros unicornis*.

7 Half of all black rhinos die from fighting.

8 If a rhino's horn breaks, it grows a new one.

Manta rays

The manta ray is one of the ocean's most mysterious giants. Here are ten essential facts about these spectacular animals.

1. Manta rays are large fish closely related to sharks.

2. A fully grown manta ray can measure seven metres wide and weigh 1,300 kilograms.

3. Rays never stop moving or they will die.

4. Despite being enormous, manta rays eat tiny creatures called zooplankton, which are often only one millimetre long!

5. Manta rays are hunted by killer whales.

6. Rays do not have bones – their skeletons are made up of tough cartilage (gristle).

7. When mantas mate, up to 30 males follow a female around trying to keep up with her as she 'dances' underwater.

8. Mantas are sometimes called devilfish because of special fins on their heads that look like evil horns.

9. To swim, mantas use their giant pectoral fins in a similar way to birds' wings. They seem to be flying through the sea in slow motion.

10. Manta rays visit special 'cleaning stations' on coral reefs to allow smaller fish to clean parasites from their skin.

Bushbabies

Galagos or bushbabies are small African mammals that are active at night. Here is a little information about these lovable primates.

→ In the Afrikaans language, bushbabies are called nagapies, which means 'little night monkeys'.

→ Bushbabies have extra-large eyes to help them see at night.

→ They have excellent hearing and their large ears help them track and catch insects in the dark.

→ Newborn bushbabies weigh only around 10–12 grams, about the same as an AAA battery.

→ Bushbabies have to be on constant watch for a variety of predators, including eagles, owls, genets and large snakes.

→ Bushbabies live in trees and are very quick and agile, being able to leap from branch to branch like squirrels.

→ A bushbaby has no nail on the second toe of each hind foot. This special toe is used for grooming.

Axolotls

The axolotl is a very peculiar amphibian, also known as the 'Mexican walking fish' (even though it's not a fish). Enjoy a handy set of facts about this rare and amazing creature.

☛ Wild axolotls are only found in one lake in Mexico called Xochimilco.

☛ Axolotls look like giant tadpoles with legs.

☛ They have strange feathery gills on the outside of their heads.

☛ If an axolotl loses an arm or leg or other body part it can grow a new one. Sometimes it even grows an extra new one!

☛ Axolotls love eating worms and will suck them into their mouths like a vacuum cleaner before swallowing them whole.

☛ Axolotls are critically endangered in the wild. This is because the lake where they live is polluted and also home to non-native fish that eat young axolotls.

☛ The Aztec people, who lived in Mexico around 500 years ago, used to like nothing better than an axolotl for lunch.

How to say 'frog' in 15 languages

Impress your friends with these worldwide
verbal variations:

- **Czech** žába
- Dutch kikker
- **Estonian** konn
- French grenouille
- **German** Frosch
- Icelandic froskur
- **Italian** rana
- Malay katak

- Maltese Żriṅġ
- **Polish** żaba
- Scots Gaelic losgann
- **Spanish** rana
- Welsh broga
- **Xhosa** isele
- Zulu frog

Migration marvels

Human beings are unusual animals because we tend to stay in one place for long periods. Many other animals need to keep moving or their food will run out – there's no supermarket delivery if you're a wildebeest!

Zebras

Zebras are not only stripy but they're often thirsty too. Since they live in hot, dry parts of Africa, they sometimes have to travel long distances to find enough drink to keep a herd of 700,000 happy. One species walks 500 kilometres to find water – that's a long way even if you're in a car!

Bar-tailed godwits

They not only have a brilliant name, but these birds are EPIC fliers. Scientists in 2007 tracked the migration of a flock of bar-tailed godwits and discovered that one flapped an incredible 11,500 kilometres *non-stop* from Alaska to New Zealand. That's a record!

Sea turtles

When baby sea turtles hatch out of their eggs, they scuttle down the beach, pop into the sea and then start swimming for years on end. Leatherback turtles make an astonishing journey of over 12,000 kilometres across the Pacific Ocean and back each year to find jellyfish to chomp. That's a meal they've really earned!

Dragonflies

Some types of dragonfly may travel over 160 kilometres a day and may make a journey from India to Africa, stopping off at islands along the way. Scientists think it takes four generations of insects to make this incredible 14,000-kilometre return trip. It would take a person over a year to walk that far!

Humpback whales

Humpback whales are not small: they're as long as 180 fish fingers and weigh the same as 50 cows. They also swim spectacular distances, migrating from cold polar waters to warm seas to breed, a distance totalling over 18,000 kilometres.

How to say 'wolf' in 14 languages

There is probably no animal with more legends attached to it than the wolf. But if you travel the globe you need to know what the locals call this howling wild canine.

- **Cherokee** — **waya**
- **Croatian** — vuk
- **Czech** — **vlk**
- **French** — loup
- **German** — **Wolf**
- **Hungarian** — farkas
- **Latvian** — **vilks**
- **Norwegian** — ulv
- **Polish** — **wilk**
- **Portuguese** — lobo
- **Spanish** — **lobo**
- **Swedish** — varg
- **Turkish** — **kurt**
- **Welsh** — blaidd

Sloths

Sloths are only found in South and Central America. They are famous for not being the speediest animals on the planet ...

The word sloth means 'lazy'.

Sloths rarely move more than 40 metres a day.

Sloths eat leaves that provide very little energy, so they keep still as much as possible.

Some sloths can extend their tongues 30 centimetres to reach their food.

Sloths are preyed on by big cats and large eagles.

Sloths allow green algae to grow on their fur, which gives them camouflage in the trees.

Sloths have long claws used to grip branches, reach food and swipe at attackers.

Many other living things live on sloths, including moths, beetles and fungi.

Female sloths give birth while hanging from trees.

Sloths climb to the ground to wee and poo. They dig a hole and cover what they have done.

There were once sloths that were as large as elephants. These supersized sloths are now extinct.

81

Friends of the pig

Domestic pigs (the ones seen on farms) have a number of wild, tusky and mean-looking cousins, including these bristly fellas:

Wild boar

These large tusked beasts eat a remarkable range of food, from roots and nuts to worms, eggs and dead animals. They're also tough, fierce and fearsomely strong.

Giant forest hog

This rare jungle pig was only discovered by scientists in 1904. It is found in Africa and can weigh up to a quarter of a tonne.

Warthog

Another African pig, this species has an enormous head, extra-long tusks and warty skin.

Bearded pig

This curious animal has long cheek hairs that look like, well, a beard. Bearded pigs live in the tropical forests of South East Asia.

Peccary

The peccary is a wild, hairy porker of Central and South America, although it is not classified as a true pig. Peccaries live in large herds, sometimes up to 100.

How to say 'otter' in 15 languages

Another opportunity to impress people around the world with your lingo flair.

Czech	**vydra**
Danish	odder
Estonian	**saarmas**
Finnish	saukko

French	**loutre**
German	Otter
Indonesia	**berang-berang**
Italian	lontra
Maori	**ota**
Scots Gaelic	dòbhran
Slovenian	**vidra**
Somali	otarka
Spanish	**nutria**
Swedish	utter
Turkish	**su samuru**

Lesser known spiders

In 2017, a group of European scientists estimated that all the world's spiders weigh around 25 million tonnes and that together they kill around 400 to 800 million tonnes of prey each year. Here are some of the planet's more unusual spider specimens:

Starbellied orbweaver

This spider has eight eyes and can produce both sticky and non-sticky threads. Orbweavers make webs with a spiral pattern.

Robber Baron Cave meshweaver

A very rare underground dweller found in only one place in the world: Robber Baron Cave in Texas, USA. This type of spider makes a tangled web on the ground.

King baboon tarantula

A 20-centimetre monster from Africa with a venomous bite. It digs burrows, can kill lizards and snakes and is a favourite snack of baboons.

Garden ghost spider

A pale, deathly-looking creepy-crawly that hunts at night and hides during the day. It's quite small.

Pirate wolf spider

With the wonderful scientific name *Pirata piraticus*, this tiny arachnid has the ability to walk on the surface of water. It does not make webs.

Peppered jumper

A mottled spider with excellent eyesight and the ability to jump when hunting. It also builds silk 'tents' to shelter in.

Hobo spider

This spider builds a funnel web in which it hides before grabbing passing prey and biting it. Fortunately, hobo spiders rarely bite people.

How many?

Nobody knows for sure how many of each kind of animal there are on Earth, especially as numbers are changing all the time, but here are some broad estimates from nature experts:

Amur leopards ··········→ **70**

Tigers ················→ **3,900**

Giant otters ···········→ **5,000**

Blue whales ············→ **25,000**

African elephants ·······→ **415,000**

Macaroni penguins ······→ **12,600,000 (12.6 million)**

Cats ····················→ **600,000,000 (600 million)**

Sheep ··················→ **1,100,000,000 (1.1 billion)**

Cattle ················→ **1,400,000,000 (1.4 billion)**

Rats ···················→ **5,000,000,000 (5 billion)**

Humans ·················→ **7,500,000,000 (7.5 billion)**

Chickens ···············→ **19,000,000,000 (19 billion)**

Fish ···················→ **3,500,000,000,000 (3.5 trillion)**

Ants ···················→ **100,000,000,000,000 (100 trillion)**

Gone forever...

Sadly, a number of animal species have become extinct, mainly because humans have destroyed their habitats or they have been hunted. Here are some animals we will never see ...

Great auk

A penguin-like bird that couldn't fly and so was easy for hunters and egg collectors to catch. It became extinct around 1850.

Desert bandicoot

Last found in 1943 in Australia, this small mammal has mysteriously vanished since.

Golden toad

A spectacularly coloured cloud forest dweller that has not been spotted since 1989.

Tasmanian tiger

Also called the thylacine, the last of these wolf-like mammals died in 1936.

Caribbean monk seal

This seal was widely hunted for centuries and has not been found since the 1950s.

Pyrenean ibex

A wild goat that died out in 2000. Attempts to clone the animals have not worked.

Quagga

Similar to the zebra, this large, striped, African animal was last seen in 1883.

How to say 'eagle' in 15 languages

Let's face it, we've all wanted to say eagle in 15 languages at some point in our lives. Well, now you can ...

- Czech — orel
- Dutch — adelaar
- Finnish — kotkar
- French — aigle
- German — Adler
- Hungarian — sas
- Irish — iolar
- Italian — aquila
- Kurdish — qertel
- Lakota — wanbli
- Polish — orzel
- Romanian — vultur
- Spanish — águila
- Swedish — örn
- Welsh — eryr

NUTTY NATURE
Wacky bats

There are, amazingly, over one thousand different types of bat. They are the only mammals that can fly and, like all mammals, have fur rather than feathers. Here are some bats with strange names and strange characteristics:

* Ghost bat – its thin pale grey wing membranes make it appear almost supernatural.
* **Sucker-footed bat – this clever beast produces a kind of gluey sweat to help it stick to smooth leaves.**
* Banana bat – a tiny bat that hides among the leaves of banana plants in the daytime.
* **New Georgian monkey-faced bat – an endangered bat that looks like a flying monkey.**
* Giant golden-crowned flying fox – a huge 'megabat' with a wingspan of 1.7 metres.
* **Little yellow bat – it's small and it's yellow and it has a wart above each eye.**
* Naked-rumped tomb bat – this bare-bottomed bat likes to live in caves and creepy tombs.
* **Hairy-legged vampire bat – it loves to suck the blood of birds and occasionally... humans!**

I can walk on water!

Like humans, most animals sink when they try to walk on water, but some don't ...

Pond skaters

These small insects have very waxy hairs on their legs. The hairs resist water and allow the skaters to skim silently over lakes and rivers.

Raft spiders

These cunning little brutes have water-repellent hairs on their bodies. The hairs stop them from sinking so that they can hunt on the surface of ponds.

Pygmy geckos

These tiny lizards, just four centimetres long, have special water-resistant skin that enables them to stand on puddles without sinking. They are also extra-light, which helps!

Western grebes

These elegant black-and-white birds perform a peculiar mating dance. A pair of grebes will beat their wings as they run across the surface of the water for some distance side by side.

Basilisk lizards

These amazing reptiles can run over rivers and lakes to catch insects. Their method is to slap their wide feet against the water while moving very fast.

Sharks to make your mind boggle

You can find over 500 kinds of shark swimming around the world's oceans. Here are some of the strangest:

HAMMERHEAD
This well-known shark has a head like a hammer and the position of its eyes give it amazing all-round vision, helping it to be a spectacular hunter.

GREENLAND SHARK
It's big, it looks brutal and it swims about as fast as a toddler walks... Yes, this cold-water monster is the world's slowest shark, cruising round the murky depths at a not-exactly-blistering 1.2 km/h!

DWARF LANTERN SHARK
It can fit in a human hand and it's also clever because it can produce its own light to attract prey in the deep, dark depths where it swims.

WOBBEGONG
This is also called a carpet shark. It has a patterned body that allows it to loiter near the ocean floor – fiendishly well camouflaged – so it can lurch up and grab unsuspecting prey passing by.

SAWSHARK
Sawsharks are small but not to be messed with because of their long thin snout with two rows of vicious teeth sticking outwards like a double-edged saw.

NERVOUS SHARK
If you are swimming in the sea and meet a shark, then hope that it's this one, because the nervous shark is terrified of humans!

Oi! Keep the noise down

You want to know about the loudest animals in the world? Here they are ...

ANIMAL	NOISE	LOUDNESS MEASURE (IN DECIBELS)	EQUAL TO
Howler monkey	Warning screeches to keep other monkeys away	90	Noisy motorbike
Coqui frog	Piercing croak to attract mates	100	Road drill
Elephant	A deep rumble to call a family member	103	Stadium crowd roar
Lion	Booming roar to establish territory	114	Live rock concert
A swarm of cicadas	Mating call produced by an internal 'drum'	120	A clap of thunder
Kakapo	The shriek of its mating call to other birds	132	A fighter jet taking off
Blue whale	An underwater siren that can be heard 800 km away	188	A rocket launch (enough to burst your eardrums)
Sperm whale	A very short 'click' to communicate to other whales	230	A destructive shock wave (fortunately it's underwater so safe)

Haven't got one!

Humans don't have wings, antlers, beaks, tails, fins or shells (at least the ones I know don't). But there are other creatures that lack some very basic features:

ANIMAL	DOESN'T HAVE
Spider	ears
Fish	neck
Snake	eyelids
Bird	teeth
Platypus	stomach
Sponge	mouth
Blind cave crab	eyes
Jellyfish	brain

Funny fungi

Just be glad you're not a fungus. Mushrooms get eaten, toadstools are trodden on and who would want to be a slime mould or some yeast that ends up in someone's sandwich? Anyway, here are a few of nature's oddest fungi:

Basket stinkhorn
It's smelly, full of holes, it's covered in goo (and usually lots of flies) and it looks like an alien Christmas decoration.

Brain mushroom
It's poisonous and it looks like someone has dropped a small brain on the forest floor.

Bearded hedgehog
This marvellous mushroom grows on trees and hangs down in white wormy danglers.

Bitter oyster
What makes this log-based fungus extra-weird is that it glows in the dark. It's lime green too!

Pixie's parasol
They're tiny (sometimes less than one centimetre across) blue, rare and look like weer sun shades made of magic ic

Small but beautiful

Some species of animal are given the title 'pygmy' to show that they are smaller than average. These are just a few examples:

Pygmy hippo
Unlike its larger cousin, this West African hippo spends a lot of time in forests.

Pygmy rabbit
The world's smallest bunny! It hides in bushes to avoid being grabbed by weasels.

Pygmy seahorse
At only two centimetres long, these minute ocean creatures blend so well into their coral surroundings that they have only recently been discovered.

Pygmy kingfisher
While most kingfishers eat fish, this very little bird mainly eats spiders, moths and grasshoppers.

Pygmy falcon
Just 19 centimetres long, this mini bird of prey is well known for pinching other birds' nests.

Pygmy owl
There are about 30 kinds of pygmy owl, many of which hunt for insects at night.

Pygmy shrew
Weighing just 1.8 grams, the Etruscan pygmy shrew is a really teeny mammal. Its heart beats about 25 times a second.

What a whiff!

Lots of animals and plants have a strong pong. Here are some of the stinkiest!

Skunk

The skunk is a famously smelly striped mammal found mainly in North America. It squirts foul-reeking chemicals out of its bottom as a defence against attackers. Its range is over three metres, so stay well away and don't annoy it!

Fulmar

Fulmars are seabirds of Northern Europe whose babies have a very nasty weapon: chick sick! When they feel threatened they vomit foul-smelling sticky stomach oil at intruders.

Hoatzin

The hoatzin is a bird from South America also known as the stinkbird. Its gut is full of bacteria used to ferment the huge amount of leaves that it eats. The result is, well ... EW!

Corpse flower

The corpse flowers of Asia are plants which attract flies by giving out the smell of rotting meat. Not the best bouquet to give your mum on Mother's Day ...

Musk ox

The musk ox is a large hairy beast found in cold northern lands. The males are pongy because they mark their territory by spraying extra-strong urine around. This whiffy wee gets matted in their dense woolly coats, giving them a stench of legendary power!

Hoopoe

The green wood hoopoe is a large and striking bird of Africa with metallic green and purple feathers. But beware if you are out bird-spotting, because its young can squirt liquid faeces when scared. Keep clear or you could get a face full of hoopoe poo-poo!

Oi, you've eaten my nest!

Did you know that some people eat birds' nests? And that those nests are made of spit? Here's the story ...

The swiftlets are birds of South East Asia that make their nests in high, dark caves.

Swiftlets have a kind of very thick saliva (spit) and they put layers of this on the walls of the caves.

The spit dries out and the layers are built up until there is a small nest, big enough to hold an egg.

When the young bird has hatched and left the nest, local people climb up the tall cliffs to reach the caves. It is a perilous journey.

They remove the old nests from the caves because they are a much prized delicacy in some countries, especially China. In fact one kilogram of these nests is worth up to 2,000 US dollars.

People eat the nests because they believe that they will help a person to stay looking and feeling young.

ODDS AND ENDS
I can fly (nearly)!

Of course birds, bats and many insects can fly long distances, but some other creatures have clever ways to move through the air as well.

Flying squirrels
This group of specialised squirrels have two furry membranes of skin called patagia (each one is a patagium) which stretch between their front and back legs. Using these built-in parachutes they can glide up to 90 metres between trees, steering with their tails.

Flying lizards
Draco lizards have wide flaps of skin attached to their ribs to allow them to glide. They even have small neck rudders to help them steer.

Flying fish
These strange fish have extra-large fins which they use like wings to jump out of the sea and glide for up to 50 metres over the water.

Flying lemurs
Also called colugos, these climbing animals have very large skin flaps extending from their necks to their tails. Using these flaps like fixed wings, they can glide over 100 metres between trees.

Lots of babies!

All animals reproduce or they would die out, and that's never a good idea. But some have more babies than others — a lot more!

Babies produced in a lifetime (average)

Human being	2
Orangutan	3
Giant panda	7
Tiger	15
Armadillo	54
Lemming	192
Rabbit	up to 360

Average litter size (babies born at once)

Walrus	1
Sun bear	2
Fox	4
Weasel	6
Mouse	7
Rat	8
Wild dog	10
Tenrec	16 (up to 30)

Egg-tastic: average number of eggs produced at once

Laysan albatross	1
Quetzal	2
Ostrich	8
Grey partridge	16
Hammerhead shark	30
Hawksbill turtle	160
Common frog	1,500
Salmon	6,000
Ghost moth	50,000
Ocean sunfish	300,000,000

Long lives and short lives

Some animals, like people, live for a long time. Others are around for only a disappointingly short while. Here are the stats:

ANIMAL	GREATEST REPORTED AGE
Polar bear	42 years
Elephant	**86 years**
Human being	122 years
Tortoise	**188 years**
Rougheye rockfish	205 years
Bowhead whale	**211 years**
Greenland shark	between 272 and 500 years
	(that's as accurate as scientists can be)
Ocean quahog	**507 years**

ANIMAL	AVERAGE LIFESPAN
Mole	3 years
Garden slug	**2 years**
House mouse	1 year
Honey bee (worker)	**6 weeks**
Mosquito (male)	10 days
Mayfly	**24 hours**

Stat attack

Which class of animal has the biggest number of species you ask? Here are the numbers of known species of nine animal classes. Of course there may be many more undiscovered species in each class too!

CLASS OF ANIMAL	EXAMPLES	NUMBER OF NAMED SPECIES (APPROX.)
Mammals	bears, mice, whales, bats	5,500
Amphibians	frogs, toads, newts, salamanders	6,500
Reptiles	lizards, turtles, snakes, crocodiles	8,700
Birds	wrens, gulls, eagles, ostriches	10,000
Fishes	salmon, ray, shark, eel	31,000
Crustaceans	crabs, shrimps, barnacles, woodlice	47,000
Molluscs	snails, slugs, clams, octopuses	85,000
Arachnids	spiders, ticks, mites, scorpions	102,000
Insects	wasps, flies, moths, beetles	1,000,000

Note: other animal classes include annelids (e.g. earthworms), echinoderms (e.g. sea urchins), diplopoda (e.g. millipedes), cnidaria (e.g. jellyfish, corals) and others that feature very tiny creatures.

Dugongs

Dugongs are rare sea mammals found mostly in warm seas such as those north of Australia. Here's what you need to know:

Dugongs can live for over 70 years.

Dugongs are often called sea cows because they eat sea-grass.

Dugongs are vegetarians.

Dugong is an Asian word meaning 'lady of the sea.'

Dugongs are up to three metres long and often weigh over half a tonne.

Dugongs were thought by sailors of olden times to be mermaids.

Dugongs do not drive buses.

Curious cats

You probably know about lions, tigers, leopards and panthers, but have you heard of these cats?

Caracal – a secretive, sandy-coloured hunter found in Africa and Asia.

Ocelot – a beautifully marked mini-leopard of South America.

Lynx – a handsome spotted cat of mainly cold places, recognised by its ear tufts.

Marbled cat – a rare small cat of the forests of South East Asia.

Serval – an African cat with extra-long legs that enable it to wade through water.

Jaguar – a large spotted cat of the Americas that can bite through the skulls of alligators.

Kodkod – a small tree-climbing feline mainly found in Chile.

Sand cat – the one cat that is found only in deserts.

Snow leopard – an endangered animal of high mountains, sometimes found at 6,000 metres above sea level.

Geoffroy's cat – a small night predator of South America, noted for standing on its hind legs.

Swarms!

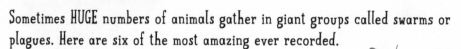

Sometimes HUGE numbers of animals gather in giant groups called swarms or plagues. Here are six of the most amazing ever recorded.

Mosquitos

Every summer in Alaska, USA, millions of small biting insects take to the air. They hatch out of swampy water and they are looking for one thing: blood to suck!

Locusts

In 1875, a weather watcher called Albert Child witnessed a truly monster cloud of these crop-munching insects in the mid-western USA. The swarm was over 160 kilometres wide. Experts have estimated that there were over 3,000,000,000,000 (three trillion) insects in the swarm.

Spiders

In 2012, land around the town of Wagga Wagga in Australia was draped in vast webs as huge armies of spiders were forced on to higher ground by rising floodwaters.

Ladybirds

In 1976, the UK was overrun by around 24 billion ladybirds. The little red beetles covered cars, pavements, trees and even people, some of whom were bitten as the insects' natural food became scarce.

Warty comb jellies

Similar to jellyfish, in the 1980s these squishy floating creatures invaded the Black Sea, eating anything small in the water. They were accidentally brought to the Black Sea by humans. Scientists made a count and discovered there were over 400 jellies in each cubic metre of water!

Yellow crazy ants

These speedy and greedy ants were introduced by humans to Christmas Island in the 1930s. Once they had devoured smaller prey they started eating the native Christmas Island crabs, overwhelming them by the sheer number of bites.

What's the difference?
Cheetah vs leopard

Lighter	**Heavier**
Can't roar	Can roar
Faster	**Not as fast**
Doesn't climb trees	Often climbs trees
Hunts mainly during the day	**Hunts mainly at night**
Has small spots	Large spots (rosettes)

What's the difference?
Turtle vs tortoise

Mostly lives in water	Lives on land
Mostly has a flat shell	Mostly has a dome-shaped shell
Webbed feet	**Short feet**
Usually lives less than 70 years	Can live over 100 years
Eats plants and animals	**Only eats plants**

What's the difference?
Alligator vs crocodile

U-shaped snout
Usually less aggressive
Only found in USA and China
Lives 40–50 years
Teeth hidden when mouth closed

V-shaped snout
Usually more aggressive
Found in many parts of the world
Lives over 70 years
Lower teeth visible when mouth closed

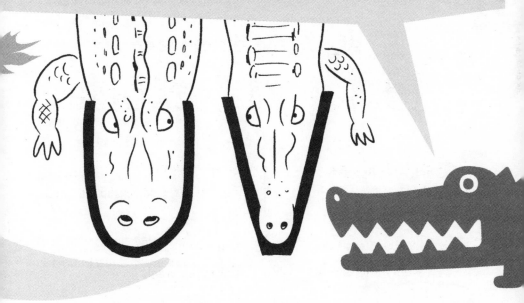

Facts about worms

The fact is that a lot of people don't know much about worms — so to prevent you from becoming one of them, here are some facts about worms!

1 Earthworms breathe through their skin – they do not have lungs.

2 An individual earthworm is both male and female.

3 Earthworms eat any plant or animal material, as long as it's dead.

4 If an earthworm is cut in half, only the head end grows into a worm again.

5 The African giant earthworm can grow up to 6.7 metres long.

6 The marine bootlace worm can grow up to 58 metres long.

7 Many worms live in the bodies of larger animals. These parasites include threadworms, tapeworms and hookworms.

8 Many beetle larvae are known as worms even though they are not really worms, e.g. glow worms and woodworms.

9 Slow worms look like snakes but are actually lizards without legs.

10 Shipworms are a type of mollusc. They have two shells that they use to bore holes in wooden boats and other objects found in the sea.

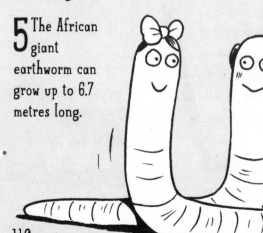

A rapid guide to moths

Moths are everywhere, but how much do you know about these varied night-flutterers?

LARGEST
The Hercules moth (wingspan 27 cm) and the Atlas moth (25 cm but heavier than the Hercules moth).

SMALLEST
Stigmella maya (wingspan 2.5 mm).

PREDATORS
Bats, owls, birds, lizards, cats and bears (among other animals).

NUMBER OF SPECIES
160,000.

FOOD
Many adult moths eat nothing, although their caterpillars may eat leaves, fruit, vegetables and wood, and some even eat carpets and woolly jumpers.

LIFESPAN
Adults: two to five weeks.

PRODUCTS
The *Bombyx mori* caterpillar is known as the silkworm because it produces silk.

ATTRACTED TO
Artificial lights (no one knows why).

Babies, babies, babies

Here are seven cute facts about animal babies.

Newborn koalas are only the size of a jellybean.

Meerkats have a babysitter system where adults take turns to teach new pups how to hide, hunt and keep clean.

Baby dolphins have special sticky tongues so they can roll them up and drink their mothers' milk without getting salt water into it.

Some chicks talk to their parents by chirping while still in the egg.

Baby elephants sometimes suck their trunks like human babies suck their thumbs.

Baby blue whales are really big — about seven metres long and three tonnes in weight!

It sometimes takes a baby penguin three days to chip its way out of its tough eggshell.

Beasty books

Many famous stories feature animals. How many of these books have you heard of? Have you read any? They are all excellent!

Book	Author	Animal(s) featured
Black Beauty	Anna Sewell	horse
White Fang	Jack London	dog
Fantastic Mr Fox	Roald Dahl	foxes
Charlotte's Web	EB White	spider, pig (and more)
The Butterfly Lion	Michael Morpurgo	lion
The Wolf Wilder	Katherine Rundell	wolves
King of the Copper Mountains	Paul Biegel	hare (and many others)
The Hodgeheg	Dick King-Smith	hedgehog
Watership Down	Richard Adams	rabbits
Varjak Paw	SF Said	cats

Animals that have caused trouble

The problem with wild animals is that they are wild – and sometimes they do cause trouble for us humans. And pets have been known to do naughty things as well. Here are six examples of animals that have caused some big trouble.

In 1994, there was nearly an international crisis when the Swedish military picked up the sounds of what they thought were Russian submarines near their coast. The noises turned out to be fish farts – herring farts, to be precise.

The great scientist Isaac Newton lost up to a year's worth of work when a manuscript he was writing burst into flames after a candle fell on it. The accident was caused by his mischievous dog, Diamond.

In 2013, a Swedish nuclear power station had to be shut down because something was blocking the vital supply of water needed to cool the hot reactor. It turned out that the blockage was the result of large clumps of jellyfish stuck in the pipes.

In 2009, people in a small town in Norway were surprised to see something hanging from an overhead electricity cable four metres up in the air one morning. It was a sheep that had got its horns trapped around the cable and then been taken on a crazy zip wire ride down the hillside until it came to a stop in the town.

In 2013, a BBC newsreader was interrupted during a live TV broadcast when something was flying around her head. It landed next to the presenter on a TV monitor for viewers to see. It was a tiny wren that had become trapped in the studio.

In 2016, the seven-billion-dollar Large Hadron Collider in Switzerland, one of the biggest pieces of scientific equipment ever built, was shut down for a week when something gnawed through an 18,000-volt power cable. It was an unfortunate stone marten (a small carnivorous mammal), which unsurprisingly didn't survive the experience.

Fantastic lizards

Lizards are found across the planet wherever temperatures are warm. They can't stand the cold! Here are quick portraits of some of the more strangely named lizards that exist on Earth:

Mangrove monitor

This hefty sea-loving lizard is over a metre long, with a polka-dot body, purple tongue and serrated teeth for munching fish. It is an excellent swimmer and often travels between islands.

Rhinoceros iguana

Found in the Caribbean, this lizard has a bony growth on its snout resembling a horn. It is another impressively large and muscular reptile, weighing up to nine kilograms. When cornered, the rhinoceros iguana will bite fiercely and lash out with its armoured tail.

Bearded dragon

The bearded dragon has amazing colour-changing spiked scales on its neck, which turn dark if it is in danger or fighting off a rival. These lizards are native to Australia and very popular around the world as pets.

Satanic leaf-tailed gecko

This truly remarkable-looking mini-lizard from the island of Madagascar has astonishing camouflage, disguising itself as a twig with old leaves to aid hunting and avoid the many predators that would like to gobble it up if only they could see it! Like other geckos, it has no eyelids and licks away dust from its eyes with a long sticky tongue.

Common scaly-foot

Since it has no legs, this very long, thin Australian lizard is often mistaken for a snake. In fact the scaly-foot (named after the scaled flaps where a lizard's legs would normally be found) flicks out its tongue when threatened so that it resembles a dangerous snake.

Panther chameleon

Chameleons are famed for being able to change colour. They also have bird-like feet for gripping trees, and eyes which can point in different directions at the same time, giving them superior dinner-spotting abilities. Panther chameleons are dotted with a wide range of colours, including blue, red, green, orange and pink.

Red-eyed crocodile skink

When the red-eyed crocodile skink is threatened by another creature, it 'freezes' its body and plays dead as a defence. Unlike most lizards, it also makes vocal sounds when in distress. This species is found in tropical forests, living on a diet of insects.

Gila monster

The gila monster has a venomous bite and so must be treated with care. It is a stout, slow, tree-climbing lizard from southern North America that mainly feeds on eggs, detecting them with its extraordinarily sensitive tongue. Amazingly, gila monsters only eat five to ten times a year.

You need to know about mould!

Mould is a kind of fungus that sometimes does astonishing things.

☞ Some moulds are used to make food. For example, certain moulds are added to soya beans to make soy sauce.

☞ Blue cheese is made by adding penicillium mould in the early stages of the cheese-making process. This type of mould is safe to eat.

☞ Moulds growing on mouldy food (such as old fruit or old bread) are definitely best avoided.

☞ Slime moulds can move towards food even though they have no brain and no feet!

☞ Some moulds have saved lives. In the past, many people died from infections caused by bacteria until Alexander Fleming discovered that some kinds of penicillium mould killed bacteria and stopped it growing. They are used in the antibiotic medicine called penicillin.

☞ Certain nasty types of mould grow in damp buildings and these can cause breathing difficulties, as well as other health problems.

PECULIAR PLANTS
Big, big, BIG tree!

The world's largest living thing is a giant sequoia tree in California, USA, known as General Sherman. Here are six full-on facts about this forest monster:

1. The tree is over 83 metres tall and 11 metres across at its base (it's as wide as a London bus is long).

2. The tree's trunk has been estimated to weigh about 1,260 tonnes: roughly the same as ten Eurotunnel locomotives.

3. It has been estimated that the tree contains enough timber to build 120 wooden houses.

4. In 1978 a branch fell off the tree – it was about 40 metres long and two metres wide. Luckily, no one was underneath when it landed ...

5. General Sherman has been growing for around 2,000 years.

6. It was named after William Sherman, a famous general in the US Civil War, who also has a tank, a fort and a monument bearing his name. It is thought that the man who discovered the tree served as a soldier with General Sherman.

The most valuable plants and fungi in the world?

Rice is probably the most valuable plant because it feeds so much of the world's population, but these little beauties cost much more for a small amount, as you'll see ...

Ginseng

This wee bush has a woody root used in Chinese traditional medicine. It's said to cure all kinds of diseases and to help, er – what was it again? – oh yes, memory. It takes six years to grow and just 100 grams can sell for more than £80.

Wasabi

Wasabi is a hard-to-grow vegetable from Japan which tastes a little like turbo-charged mustard. It only grows well in streams with very clean water, and just 40 grams of stem costs £10.

Orchids

These strange, elegant flowers are highly prized, depending on how rare they are. A Gold of Kinabalu orchid once sold for £3,800!

Saffron

Saffron is a small crocus flower. The teeny red filaments in the centre of the flowers have to be plucked out (with great difficulty) then dried. They are used as a flavouring and to colour food yellow. Ten grams costs about £35. Ten grams is about the weight of a large coin.

Here are two valuable fungi. Fungi are not plants and they're not animals either, in case you didn't know.

Oyster mushrooms

They're flat, they're grey and they're yummy (well, to some people). One kilogram will set you back about £15.

Truffles

Truffles are a rare type of fungus regarded as one of the world's greatest foods. Most of them look like small round lumps of coal but a 50-gram black truffle can sell for about £160.

Useful things made from plants

Most people know that paper is made from trees, but did you know that these things are also made from plants?

RUBBER GLOVES
latex trees

WINE CORKS
cork oak

CHOCOLATE
cacao tree

CELLOPHANE
various plants such as cotton

ASPIRIN
willow tree

BEER
barley and hops

DOORMATS
coconuts

LOO PAPER
various trees

Built from ... plants!

Wood is plant material that is used for building all sorts of things, from boats to churches — but did you know about the remarkable uses of these plants? Read on ...

PLANT	WHAT IT CAN BE USED FOR
Reeds	To make thatched roofs.
Straw *	For insulating walls to keep heat inside.
Bamboo	In India and many other countries, bamboo is used to construct scaffolding and bridges.
Cotton	Cotton has been used for centuries to make tents, sails and shelters.
Waste sugar cane	The cellulose from plants can be moulded into any shape and hardened to make products like beams, boards and doors.
Manila hemp	The fibres from its leaves are very strong and can be made into items like rope, fishing nets and carpets.
Palm leaves	Palm leaves can be made into furniture, plates and even hut walls.
Grass	Some traditional houses in Norway have roofs covered in living grass.
Coir	The fibres from coconut husks can be made into lots of things, including floor tiles.
Tree bark	Used to build canoes in Canada.

* Straw is the dried stalks of cereal plants such as barley, maize, oats, rice and wheat.

Plants that give us spices

The world loves spicy food! But there would be no curries, chilli con carne or Cajun recipes without a special group of plants that provide us with these zingy flavourings.

Black pepper

This is made from the dried fruit of a vine grown in India and countries in South East Asia. Black pepper is the world's most traded spice and an essential ingredient for every cook.

Ginger

Ginger is the swollen root of a large plant from Asia. It has been used for centuries to make drinks, sweets and spicy mixtures, and as a favourite baking ingredient as well as hot savoury dishes.

Cloves

Cloves are the dried flower buds of a tree that is native to parts of Indonesia and South East Asia. As well as adding a kick to food, cloves are traditionally used to ease toothache.

Turmeric

This yellow spice is made from the dried underground stem of a plant from Asia. The turmeric plant is boiled for some time then dried in ovens and finally ground into a golden powder. It has been used as a dye and a medicine as well as for cooking.

Coriander

Powdered coriander is made from the ground-up seeds of a tall green herb that grows in warm countries around the world. Fresh coriander is the leaves of the plant.

Nutmeg

A nutmeg is a large dried seed of a type of tree that grows naturally on only a few islands in Indonesia. It is usually grated and used to flavour both sweet and savoury dishes.

Cinnamon

This is the dried inner bark of a tree growing mainly in South East Asia. Stems are grown and cut and the outer bark is scraped off. Next the inner bark used for cinnamon is removed by beating the branch with a hammer. It is then dried and sold in curled sections or ground into powder and used to flavour desserts and spicy savoury dishes.

Chilli powder

This famously fiery red food is made from the dried fruit of chilli pepper plants, originally from Mexico. These fruit contain chemicals that give them a powerful 'hot' spiciness.

The world's rarest plants

If you find one of these, then you have made an outstanding discovery, because there are hardly any left on the planet.

Attenborough's pitcher plant

This beauty was only discovered in 2007 on a mountain in the Philippines. It is a carnivorous plant that traps small animals, including shrews, in its liquid-filled cup.

Golf ball

This mysterious cactus from Mexico not only looks like a golf ball but also has amazing flowers. People have dug them up illegally, meaning that only very few survive.

Coral tree

There are fewer than 50 of these amazing red-flowered trees left in the forests of Tanzania in east Africa.

Jellyfish tree

This bush from the Seychelles was thought to be extinct until someone found one in the 1970s. It has strange fruit that look like jellyfish.

Poke-me-boy

This tiny spiky shrub grows on a few low-lying islands in the Caribbean Sea. It could die out forever if ocean levels rise.

A little coconut information!

You probably know something about coconuts already,
but here's a chance to find out even more ...

❁ Coconuts grow on tall trees called coconut palms.

❁ Coconuts are not nuts (they are fruit).

❁ Spanish sailors from around **500** years ago thought that the fruit
looked like a human head so they named it 'coco', meaning face.

❁ Dried white coconut flesh, called copra, is used to make
coconut oil. It is classed as dangerous goods because it can
heat up when stored and ignite, causing fires.

❁ Coconuts have a hard outer husk covered in fibres
which are used to make rope and brushes.

❁ In Thailand, monkeys are trained to collect coconuts from trees.

❁ Coconut palm leaves grow up to six metres long (that's a BIG leaf).

❁ The sugary sap of the tree is used to make drinks, syrup and
sweets in Asian and Pacific Island countries.

Some unusual fruits

Most people know about apples, bananas, strawberries and peaches, but not so many have tasted these less famous fruity beauties:

Cloudberry
A small plant of cold places. Its fruit is used to flavour puddings in Sweden and Norway.

Miracle fruit
An African berry which, when eaten, makes sour foods like lemons taste sweet.

Monstera
Also called the Swiss cheese plant because it has holes in its leaves. The fruit is extra sweet.

Wax jambu
A fruit from tropical islands which can be white, green, red, purple or black!

Custard apple
A fruit of tropical countries, which tastes like custard and is also known as ox-heart.

Dead man's fingers
A plant with long edible pods – sometimes called blue sausage fruit.

Blue tongue
A small berry-like fruit which stains the tongue blue when eaten.

Lilly pilly
An Australian tree which produces clusters of pink-red berries used to make jam.

Dragon fruit
A cactus from Mexico with fruit that look like props from a sci-fi film.

Durian
A large spiky fruit famed for its powerful pong which many people find repulsive. It is banned from buses and trains in some countries.

129

THINGS TO DO

Quiz: bird, mammal or fish?

OK, prepare to have your animal knowledge put to the test in this juicy three-level quiz. Can you beat your friends and family? Simply say (or write) if each animal is a bird, mammal or fish.

Answers on page 154.

LEVEL: TRICKY		LEVEL: TOUGH		LEVEL: WHAAATTT!	
1.	dory	1.	civet	1.	ayu
2.	marlin	2.	koi	2.	quoll
3.	gibbon	3.	dunnock	3.	saki
4.	blenny	4.	tetra	4.	frogmouth
5.	quail	5.	ibex	5.	zokor
6.	jay	6.	beluga	6.	panga
7.	hornbill	7.	kookaburra	7.	rock beauty
8.	walrus	8.	ibis	8.	olingo
9.	sandpiper	9.	slimehead	9.	noddy
10.	mongoose	10.	bandicoot	10.	knot

Monkey puzzle

Which is a real monkey and which is not? One of each pair is genuine. Answers on page 154.

1. golden monkey or aluminium monkey?

2. trousered macaque or booted macaque?

3. yellow baboon or purple baboon?

4. drill or hammer?

5. black-headed marmoset or black-bottomed marmoset?

6. bearded tamarin or moustached tamarin?

7. two-striped day monkey or three-striped night monkey?

8. Barbara Brown's titi or Barbara Brown's tutu?

9. bald saki or hairy saki?

10. yellow-tailed woolly monkey or woolly-tailed yellow monkey?

Animal riddles

Riddles are little word puzzles that often have a trick in them. Can you solve these? The answers are on page 155.

1. Which lion has eyes and teeth but no mane, no claws and no legs?

2. What's on your head that runs off when it's frightened?

3. What has wings and a handle?

4. What has a nose like a tree, legs like a tree and a tail like a branch?

5. What wears a thick coat in winter and pants in summer?

6. What hops when it walks and sits when it stands?

7. What grows down as it grows up?

Chinchilla mini-quiz

How many of these multiple-choice answers can you get right? Can you outscore a friend? Answers on page 155.

1. What type of animal is a chinchilla?
a) Reptile
b) Bird
c) Mammal

2. Where do wild chinchillas come from?
a) South America
b) Europe
c) The North Pole

3. Why do chinchillas have very thick fur?
a) For camouflage
b) They live in cold mountains
c) To make themselves look larger

4. Which of these animals hunts chinchillas?
a) Snake
b) Vole
c) Wallaby

5. Why are chinchillas endangered in the wild?
a) Loss of habitat
b) People catching them for fur
c) Disease

6. How do chinchillas keep themselves clean?
a) They dip themselves in water
b) They roll in dust
c) They lick their fur

Quiz: reptile, insect or crustacean?

Here is another sneaky three-level quiz. Can you beat your friends and family? Simply say (or write) if each animal is a reptile, insect or crustacean. Answers on page 155.

LEVEL: HMMM

1. turtle
2. wasp
3. shrimp
4. crab
5. ant
6. cobra
7. moth
8. alligator
9. dragonfly
10. crayfish

LEVEL: OO-ER

1. lobster
2. mosquito
3. cricket
4. iguana
5. chameleon
6. mamba
7. shield bug
8. prawn
9. python
10. weevil

LEVEL: EEK!

1. krill
2. cockroach
3. gecko
4. mantis
5. monitor
6. glow worm
7. barnacle
8. skink
9. woodlouse
10. gavial

Odd one out!

Can you spot the odd one out in each list of animals? Answers on page 156.

1.
YAK
WHALE
EEL
SQUID

2.
RAT
GORILLA
LION
SQUIRREL

3.
LIZARD
TOAD
TURTLE
SNAKE

4.
FLEA
ANT
GRASSHOPPER
SPIDER

5.
EMU
FROG
ALLIGATOR
FOX

6.
KOALA
KANGAROO
TASMANIAN DEVIL
WOLF

7.
TANG
TROUT
TOUCAN
TURBOT

8.
WASP
STONEFISH
SCORPION
VIPER

Bird brain

This is a good memory game and is fun
to play in the car. Any number can join in
and it doesn't need any paper or pens.

Try playing the 'I went
to the zoo ...' version
so that you can
include any animal!

1 Everyone pretends they're on a bird-spotting trip. Choose
someone to go first. This person says which bird they saw,
for example, a buzzard. The person should say,
'I went bird-spotting and I saw a buzzard.'

2 The second person must repeat what the first person said
then add their own bird, for example,
'I went bird-spotting and I saw a buzzard
and a robin.'

3 The next person repeats what person two said
then adds their own bird, for example, 'I went
bird-spotting and I saw a buzzard, a robin and
an oystercatcher.'

4 Continue with everyone taking
turns until someone is stuck.
That person is then out and
the others carry on until
there is a winner.

You can also play the game
alphabetically: each new bird
must begin with the next letter
of the alphabet for example,
'I went bird-spotting and I saw
an albatross, a bullfinch, a crow,
a dove ...' etc.

Quiz: lions true or false

Are these statements about lions true or are they made-up waffle? Let's see what you know! Answers on page 156.

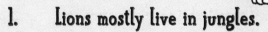

1. Lions mostly live in jungles.

2. The lion is the largest big cat.

3. Female lions are heavier than male lions.

4. Lions usually live longer in zoos than in the wild.

5. Female lions hunt more often than males.

6. All wild lions are found in Africa.

7. Lions sleep for around three-quarters of each day.

8. A lion can eat a whole buffalo in one go.

Initial challenge

This is a pen and paper game. Any number can play and you can even do it on your own.

1 The idea is to think of animals with short names, for example, cat, newt, bee.

2 You choose one and write the name vertically on the left-hand side of the paper:

B
A
T

3 You then need to try and describe or sum up that animal using words beginning with each letter of its name, for example:

B : Brown	Bold	Brilliant
A : And	At	At
T : Tiny	Twilight	Twisting

4 Think of your own animals, write down your ideas and then each read out your best one.

5 Here are some animals to try:

- ant
- crab
- dog
- owl
- frog
- hare
- lion
- wasp
- rat
- seal
- fly
- swan
- bear
- ape

6 For a bigger challenge, try animals with longer names!

Guess my creature

This is an animal guessing game for any number of people.

1. The oldest person goes first. He or she thinks of an animal that everyone playing will know. It can be any kind of animal.

2. The rest of the group then ask questions to try and discover the mystery animal.

3. The questions can only be answered yes or no. So you cannot ask, 'How many legs does it have?' or even 'What kind of animal is it?' But you can ask questions like:
- Is it a bird?
- Does it have fur?
- Is it as big as a cat?

4. The best kinds of questions will probably be about what it looks like.

Here is an example (the mystery animal is a frog):

Q. Is it a mammal?
A. No

Q. Can it fly?
A. No

Q. Does it have four legs?
A. Yes

Q. Is it covered in fur?
A. No

Q. Is it a reptile?
A. No

Q. Is it green?
A. Yes

And so on!

Animal chains

This is a fun game for two or more people. You don't need anything to play it.

1 The youngest person goes first and says an animal for example, 'camel'.

2 The next person must say an animal starting with the last letter of the previous animal. Camel ends with an L so this person could say 'lapwing', for example.

3 The next person's animal must begin with G because lapwing ends in G.

4 A player who is stuck is out. Continue until only the winner is left. Younger children can be paired with an adult.

5 You can also play the game with one type of animal for example, fish or mammal. Or for a bigger challenge, try plants instead. (Remember, trees are plants!)

Plant quiz

Here's a short quiz that you can do and then try out on someone else. Who can get the best score in your family? Answers are on page 157.

1. What's the tallest grass in the world? (Clue: you can make furniture from it.)

3. What is the world's heaviest fruit? (Clue: you might think it's a vegetable.)

4. Which insect-eating plant is named after a goddess? (Clue: it's also named after a planet.)

5. What piece of sports equipment is traditionally made from the wood of the willow tree? (Clue: players usually wear a white kit when they use it.)

2. What is the main product made from the pods of the cacao tree? (Clue: it's most people's favourite sweet treat.)

Nature natter

This is another talking game, good for playing on a long journey. In this game no one is out and it can be played by any number of people.

1.
Each person in turn says an animal beginning with A.

2.
Keep going until a player gets stuck. You can have as many turns as possible.

3.
When someone is stuck on A, that person can then say an animal beginning with B. Everyone then takes turns to say animals beginning with B until a player gets stuck again.

4.
The idea is to name as many animals as you can right through the alphabet.

5.
Remember to include insects, fish, birds and reptiles!

Animal name game

Here is something to do with friends or family on a rainy day. If you are daring you can even play it on a day when it's not raining! You need a piece of paper and a pen each.

1. Each person writes the alphabet down the left-hand side of the paper.

2. On 'Go!' everyone must try to write one animal beginning with each letter of the alphabet. It can be any kind of animal.

3. When the first person has finished, he or she says, 'Stop!'

4. Score your answers like this:
• You get two points for each animal no one else has got.
• You get one point if someone else has the same animal as you.
• You don't get any points if you missed a letter.

5. Add up the scores to find the winner.

6. You can play lots of different versions of this game:
• Put a time limit on for example, ten minutes (you can use a mobile phone timer for this).
• Just do one type of animal for example, bird.
• Try the game with plants.
• Allow more than one answer for each letter.

Not-so-cuddly quiz

Some animals are cute and cuddly and some are more of the growly, stingy, snappy kind. How many of these can you get right? Answers on page 157.

1. Which of these is a large fish that can give you a big zapping shock if you get too close?

Electric eel or eland

2. Which of these is a large river-dwelling reptile, very similar to a crocodile?

Caiman or caribou

3. Which of these is a fast and deadly venomous snake?

Taipan or tetra

4. Which of these is a giant bird with a vicious kick and a giant slicing toe claw?

Caracal or cassowary

5. Which of these is a large shaggy mammal with pickaxe claws?

Skink or sloth bear

6. Which of these is like a monster wasp with an extremely painful sting?

Hyena or hornet

7. Which of these is a tiny bug which burrows into its victim's skin and then has a bloodsucking feast?

Toucan or tick

8. Which of these is a spider with a bite that will do you no good at all?

Redback or raccoon

9. Which of these is a jellyfish with 24 stinging tentacles two metres long?

Sea nettle or sea slug

10. Which of these is an innocent-looking bird with a dagger-like beak that can be used to spear fish?

Loon or lemur

JOKES AND RIDDLES

Tree jokes

How come a moose can jump higher than a tree?
Trees can't jump.

How do trees get on the internet?
They log on.

What did the palm tree say to the beech tree?
Nothing. Trees can't talk.

What looks like half an oak tree?
The other half.

Which side of a tree has the most branches?
The outside.

What has six legs and 100,000 leaves?

A tree – I lied about the legs.

146

Colourful gags

What's bored and grey?
⊙ A seal in a chemistry exam.

What's itchy and red?
⊙ A ladybird in a new cardigan.

What's pink and noisy?
⊙ A flamingo with a road drill.

What's yellow and impatient?
⊙ A budgie at traffic lights.

What's happy and white?
⊙ A snow goose on a lilo.

Pun fun

✪ **What's the biggest noise in the ocean?**
A wail.

✪ **Which bird does things just for fun?**
A lark.

✪ **Which animal comes in strawberry, chocolate and lemon?**
A moose.

✪ **Which animal can you wash your hands in?**
A bison.

✪ **Which animal never wears clothes?**
A bear.

✪ **Which bird keeps very low?**
A duck.

147

Fun riddles

These nature riddles are a little bit silly but not as hard as the last set! Answers on page 157.

1. What has lots of blades but is not dangerous?

2. What is rounded yet sharp?

3. What is hairy, lives in trees and is good at keeping still?

4. What has five arms, no legs and no head?

5. What animal swims in the ocean but has no fins?

6. What animal is faster than a greyhound, stronger than an elephant and flies higher than an eagle?

Animal funnies

Why do bears have fur coats?
They don't like anoraks.

Where does a lion stand in a bus queue?
Anywhere it likes.

Why do penguins eat fish?
You try finding sandwiches in the ocean.

Where do giraffes learn how to find food?
At high school.

What did the pigeon say when it laid a square egg?
Ouch!

Why didn't the sparrow use the bird table?
It was waiting for some chairs.

More nature jokes

Why are rhinos wrinkly?

They don't like being ironed.

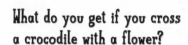

What do you get if you cross a crocodile with a flower?

I don't know but I'm not going to smell it!

What do you call an elephant in a shower cubicle?

Stuck.

When is it bad luck to see a black cat?

When you're a mouse.

What do you give a hippo that's feeling sick?

Plenty of room.

Gnarly nature riddles

These riddles are extra tough! Look at every piece of information and try to work them out. There are extra clues to help.
Answers on page 158.

1. What wriggles, sleeps and flaps in one year?
(Clue: they're colourful garden visitors.)

2. What falls, breaks, grows and lives again?
(Clue: it's a part of a plant.)

3. What dangles, spins, waits and pounces?
(Clue: it's often black.)

4. What rises, opens, flies away and begins again?
(Clue: it's a well-known weed.)

5. What is beautiful, sharp, colourful and a good climber?
(Clue: they usually smell lovely.)

6. What's in armour but not at war and hides when danger is near?
(Clue: they move slowly.)

7. What has brown inside white inside green?
(Clue: you've probably eaten lots of these.)

151

Wacky picture puzzles

Do you know what these are? There's a nature connection with each one (warning: they're VERY silly). If 1 is a 'great white envelope', what are the others?

Answers on page 158.

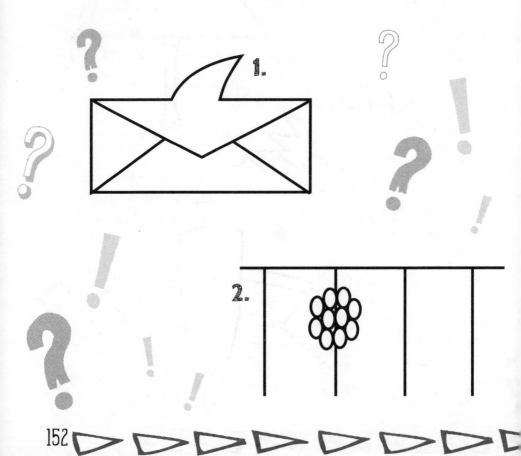

1.

2.

3.

4.

5.

6.

Answers

Quiz: bird, mammal or fish? page 130

LEVEL: TRICKY

1. dory — F
2. marlin — F
3. gibbon — M
4. blenny — F
5. quail — B
6. jay — B
7. hornbill — B
8. walrus — M
9. sandpiper — B
10. mongoose — M

LEVEL: TOUGH

1. civet — M
2. koi — F
3. dunnock — B
4. tetra — F
5. ibex — M
6. beluga — M
7. kookaburra — B
8. ibis — B
9. slimehead — F
10. bandicoot — M

LEVEL: WHAAATTT!

1. ayu — F
2. quoll — M
3. saki — M
4. frogmouth — B
5. zokor — M
6. panga — F
7. rock beauty — F
8. olingo — M
9. noddy — B
10. knot — B

Monkey puzzle

page 131

1. golden monkey
2. booted macaque
3. yellow baboon
4. drill
5. black-headed marmoset
6. moustached tamarin
7. three-striped night monkey
8. Barbara Brown's titi
9. bald saki
10. yellow-tailed woolly monkey

Animal riddles

page 132
1. A sea lion
2. A hare
3. A bat
4. An elephant
5. A wolf (or a dog)
6. A kangaroo
7. A duck or a bird (the soft, fluffy feathers on a young bird are called down)

Chinchilla mini-quiz

page 133
1. Mammal
2. South America
3. They live in cold mountains
4. Snake
5. People catching them for fur
6. They roll in dust

Quiz: reptile, insect or crustacean?

page 134

LEVEL: HMMM

1. turtle   R
2. wasp   I
3. shrimp   C
4. crab   C
5. ant   I
6. cobra   R
7. moth   I
8. alligator   R
9. dragonfly   I
10. crayfish   C

LEVEL: OO-ER

1. lobster   C
2. mosquito   I
3. cricket   I
4. iguana   R
5. chameleon   R
6. mamba   R
7. shield bug   I
8. prawn   C
9. python   R
10. weevil   I

LEVEL: EEK!

1. krill   C
2. cockroach   I
3. gecko   R
4. mantis   I
5. monitor   R
6. glow worm   I
7. barnacle   C
8. skink   R
9. woodlouse   C
10. gavial   R

Odd **one** out!

page 135

1. yak (the only land animal –
the others live in water)
2. gorilla (the only animal with
no tail)
3. toad (the only amphibian –
the others are reptiles)
4. spider (the only one which isn't
an insect)
5. emu (the only one with two legs)
6. wolf (the only one which is not a
marsupial – an animal with a pouch)
7. toucan (the only bird – the others
are fish)
8. viper (the only one which does
not have a sting – it has a
venomous bite)

Quiz: lions true or false

page 137

1. F (lions mostly live in grasslands)
2. F (the tiger is the largest cat)
3. F (male lions are heavier)
4. T (lions live longer in zoos,
on average)
5. T (females do most of the hunting)
6. F (some lions are found in India)
7. T (lions mostly hunt at dusk or
at night)
8. F (lions can eat a lot of meat but
not that much!)

Plant quiz
page 141
1. bamboo
2. chocolate
3. pumpkin
4. Venus flytrap
5. cricket bat

Not-so-cuddly quiz
pages 144-145
1. electric eel
2. caiman
3. taipan
4. cassowary
5. sloth bear
6. hornet
7. tick
8. redback
9. sea nettle
10. loon

Fun riddles
page 148
1. grass
2. a hedgehog
3. a coconut
4. a starfish
5. a penguin
6. a human (in a jet aircraft)

Gnarly nature riddles

page 151
1. A butterfly
2. A seed
3. A spider
4. A dandelion
5. A rose
6. A tortoise
7. An apple

Wacky picture puzzles

page 152

1. Great white envelope
2. Badly parked raspberry
3. Pizza delivery mouse
4. Elephant sandwich
5. Loch Ness hedgehog
6. World's strongest carrot

FURTHER INFORMATION

Books to read

These books have more nature information, facts and fun:

SuperNature (DK Nature) by Derek Harvey (Dorling Kindersley, 2012)

Natural History Museum Book of Animal Records by Mark Carwardine (Natural History Museum Press, 2013)

Weird But True: Animals (National Geographic Kids, 2018)

Animal Activity by Isabel Thomas (Bloomsbury, 2017)

Websites

Where to find out more wild and wacky information about the world of wildlife:

BBC Earth www.bbc.com/earth/uk – loads of information and amazing video clips

National Geographic Kids www.natgeokids.com/uk – fun facts, quizzes and competitions

RSPB fun facts and interesting articles www.rspb.org.uk/birds-and-wildlife/read-and-learn/fun-facts-and-articles/ – find out loads of fun facts and interesting articles.

CBBC www.bbc.co.uk/cbbc/topics/animals – funny videos, amazing facts and quizzes

The RSPB is the UK's largest nature conservation charity, inspiring everyone to give nature a home. Together with their partners, the RSPB protects threatened birds and wildlife so our towns, coast and countryside will teem with life once again. They also play a leading role in a worldwide partnership of nature conservation organisations.

ALSO BY ANDY SEED:

This laugh-out-loud book is bursting with silly lists, facts, jokes and funny true stories all about animals, inventions, food and much more. Find out about The Great Stink, the man who ate a bike, the world's richest cat and a sofa that can do 101 mph. Unmissable!

WINNER OF BEST BOOK WITH FACTS IN THE BLUE PETER BOOK AWARDS

£5.99 ISBN 978-1-4088-5079-4

£5.99
ISBN 978-1-4088-5338-2

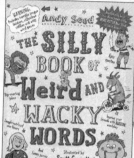

Have hours of fun wixing your mords with this hilarious book, packed full of funny rhymes, puns, games, jokes, gibberish and more. Find out wacky nicknames, learn some rude place names, get your teeth around terrible tongue twisters and laugh at some brilliantly silly lingo.

Andy Seed's laugh-out-loud 'Anti-Boredom' series has something for everyone. A seemingly endless car journey? A boring rainy afternoon? A dull holiday? Hours and hours outdoors? Or even a boring time in the run-up to Christmas?
Andy's got an activity, a joke or a game for that! These witty and wacky books are bursting with funny facts, games, quizzes and things to do for hours of fun.

£5.99
ISBN 978-1-4088-5076-3
ISBN 978-1-4088-7010-5
ISBN 978-1-4088-7009-9

160